Chapter 1: Introduction to Swimming
- The history of swimming and its evolution.
- The importance of swimming for physical and mental health.
- Types of swimming (recreational, competitive, and lifesaving).

Chapter 2: Preparing to Learn Swimming
- Choosing the right equipment (swimsuits, goggles, caps).
- Getting familiar with swimming facilities (public and private pools).
- Tips for safety and water security.

Chapter 3: Overcoming the Fear of Water

- Causes of fear of water and how to overcome it.
- Relaxation and breathing techniques.
- Simple exercises to adjust to the water.

Chapter 4: Swimming Basics
- The correct body position in the water.
- Basic breathing techniques.
- Balance and floating in the water.

Chapter 5: Learning Basic Strokes
- Freestyle swimming (front crawl).
- Breaststroke.
- Backstroke.
- Butterfly stroke (simple introduction).

Chapter 6: Developing Skills
- Improving speed and efficiency.
- Turning techniques at the pool edge.
- Endurance and strength training exercises.

Chapter 7: Avoiding Common Mistakes
- Incorrect body position.
- Irregular breathing.
- Uncoordinated movements.

Chapter 8: Swimming as Part of a Healthy Lifestyle
- Integrating swimming into the daily routine.
- Its benefits for physical and mental health.
- Ways to maintain motivation and continuous improvement.

Chapter 1: Introduction to Swimming

1.1 The History of Swimming and Its Evolution

Swimming is one of the oldest activities practiced by humans, dating back to ancient times. Stone carvings discovered in Egypt, dating from 2500 BC, show people swimming. It was also practiced by Greek and Roman civilizations as part of their military training programs and as a recreational activity.

During the Middle Ages, swimming declined in popularity in Europe but remained an important part of daily life in Asia and the Middle East. In the 19th century, swimming began to resurface as a competitive sport with organized competitions in England.

Today, swimming is an Olympic sport and a globally popular activity that combines recreation, fitness, and competition.

1.2 The Importance of Swimming for Physical and Mental Health

Swimming is a comprehensive physical activity that improves various bodily functions. Here are some key health benefits:

- **Cardiovascular Strengthening:** Swimming improves the efficiency of the circulatory system and reduces the risk of heart disease.
- **Muscle Strength and Flexibility:** Since swimming targets various muscle groups, it enhances muscle strength and flexibility.
- **Calorie Burning:** Swimming is an effective way to lose weight and burn

calories.
- **Mental Health Benefits:** Swimming helps reduce stress and anxiety thanks to the calming effects of water, and it improves mood.

1.3 Types of Swimming
There are different forms of swimming, each serving various purposes:

1. **Recreational Swimming:**
   - The main goal is enjoyment and relaxation.
   - Suitable for all ages and skill levels.
2. **Competitive Swimming:**
   - Includes races in various swimming styles, such as freestyle, breaststroke, butterfly, and backstroke.
   - Requires intensive training to improve speed and technique.
3. **Lifesaving Swimming:**
   - Used in emergency situations to save others.
   - Involves special techniques for rescuing and safely transporting individuals.

1.4 Why Should You Learn Swimming?
Learning to swim is not just a sports skill; it is a life-saving necessity. Swimming provides vital skills that could save one's life or the life of others in critical situations. It also boosts self-confidence and offers opportunities for personal development, whether in a health, recreational, or competitive context.

This chapter provides the foundation for understanding the significance and history of swimming, setting the learner on the path to confidently acquire swimming skills.

Chapter 2: Preparing to Learn Swimming

2.1 Choosing the Right Equipment
When you begin learning to swim, it's important to ensure you are equipped with the proper gear for comfort and safety. Here are the key items you will need:

1. **Swimwear:**
   - Choose comfortable swimwear made from flexible, quick-drying materials.
   - For men: Tight-fitting or loose-fitting swim trunks, depending on preference.
   - For women: One-piece or two-piece swimsuits, based on comfort.
2. **Goggles:**
   - Protect your eyes from the chlorine in pool water.
   - Make sure to select goggles that fit your face comfortably and provide clear vision underwater.

3. **Swim Cap:**
    - Used to reduce water resistance and keep your hair clean.
    - Made from materials like silicone, latex, or fabric.

4. **Additional Tools (Optional):**
    - **Earplugs:** To prevent water from entering the ears.
    - **Nose Clips:** To prevent water from entering the nose while swimming.

2.2 Getting Familiar with Swimming Facilities

Before you start learning to swim, it's essential to get familiar with your surroundings. Swimming facilities vary in design and rules, so consider the following:

1. **Types of Pools:**
   - **Public Pools:** Often crowded but suitable for learning to swim as they typically have instructors and training programs.
   - **Private Pools:** Offer a quieter environment but may come at a higher cost.
2. **Pool Design:**
   - Familiarize yourself with the pool's depth and areas designated for deep and shallow swimming.
   - Ensure safety features like protective barriers or lane dividers are in place.
3. **Safety Rules:**
   - Follow the instructions of instructors and lifeguards.

- Confirm the availability of emergency equipment, such as life rings.

2.3 Water Safety Tips
Water safety is a top priority when learning to swim. Here are some tips to follow:

1. **Stay Close to the Edges:**
   - As a beginner, try to stay in shallow areas or near the pool's edge to avoid feeling uncomfortable.
2. **Learn Emergency Signals:**
   - Make sure you understand the signals used to indicate issues such as needing help or stopping swimming.
3. **Swim Under Supervision:**
   - It's best to have someone experienced or a coach with you to assist during learning.
4. **Take Breaks When Needed:**
   - If you feel tired or lose focus, take a break to rest.

2.4 Preparing the Right Mindset
Developing a positive mindset is an important part of preparing to learn

swimming.
- **Embrace Mistakes:** Swimming requires time and practice, so don't be afraid to make mistakes.
- **Focus on Consistency:** Don't expect to master swimming in a single day. Take small, steady steps.
- **Self-Motivation:** Set small goals and celebrate achieving them. This will help you stay motivated.

This chapter comprehensively prepares the learner to begin swimming by providing necessary equipment and outlining basic safety principles

Chapter 3: Overcoming the Fear of Water

3.1 Understanding the Causes of Fear of Water

Fear of water is a common feeling, especially among those who haven't been exposed to swimming in their childhood or who have had negative experiences with water.

This fear can stem from:
- **Past Negative Experiences:** Such as drowning or feeling a lack of control in the water.
- **Fear of the Unknown:** Not being able to see or understand what's happening beneath the surface of the water.
- **Lack of Exposure:** Limited experience or interaction with water since childhood.

Understanding these causes is the first step toward overcoming the fear and building confidence in the water.

3.2 Relaxation and Breathing Techniques
The ability to relax and breathe properly is essential in overcoming the fear of water. You can try these techniques:

1. **Deep Breathing:**
    - Stand near the edge of the pool or in a shallow area.
    - Inhale slowly through your nose, hold the breath for a few seconds, and then exhale slowly through your mouth.
    - Repeat this process to reduce tension and calm your heartbeat.
2. **Relaxation Exercises in Water:**

- Sit or stand in a shallow area where you feel safe.
- Let the water gradually cover your feet or legs.
- Move slowly in the water to feel comfortable and get accustomed to the texture and temperature of the water.

3. **Floating Exercises:**
   - Gently lie on your back, supported by another person or using flotation devices such as a kickboard.
   - Focus on breathing and relaxing while floating, which helps build confidence that the water can support your body.

3.3 Practical Steps to Adjust to the Water
To overcome the fear, it is necessary to take gradual steps that make both the body and mind more comfortable with the aquatic environment:

1. **Submerging the Face in Water:**
   - Start by submerging your face in the water for a few

seconds and then lifting it back out.
- You can begin by submerging your mouth and nose first, before progressing to fully submerging your face.
- Try opening your eyes underwater with swim goggles to see the world beneath the surface and feel more secure.

2. **Bubble Exercises:**
   - Take a deep breath, submerge your face in the water, and blow air out of your mouth to form bubbles.
   - Repeat this several times to increase comfort in the water and develop better breath control.

3. **Trying Simple Movements:**
   - Once you feel comfortable with your face in the water, try moving your arms and legs slowly.
   - Use flotation devices like kickboards to practice

movements without the fear of sinking.

3.4 Tips for Building Confidence

• **Start Slowly:** Don't push yourself to progress too quickly. Learning to swim takes time and patience.

• **Seek Support:** Swimming with friends or family members who are experienced can give you a sense of security.

• **Focus on Small Progress:** Celebrate any achievement, no matter how small, such as being able to submerge your face or float.

• **Self-Motivation:** Remind yourself of the reasons you want to learn swimming, like improving your health or enjoying time with family.

3.5 When to Seek Professional Help
If the fear of water persists despite your own efforts, it might be beneficial to consult a professional swim coach.
• Qualified instructors have experience working with people who are afraid of water.
• They can provide a safe learning environment and offer tailored training suited to your needs.

This chapter focuses on building confidence through simple and effective techniques to overcome fear, paving the way for progress in learning swimming with peace of mind.

Chapter 4: Swimming Fundamentals

4.1 Correct Body Position in Water
The correct body position is essential for effective swimming. Proper posture helps improve buoyancy, reduce water resistance, and conserve energy.

1. **Horizontal Body Position:**

- Your body should be flat and extended horizontally on the surface of the water.
- Keep your head in a proper alignment, so your eyes are looking downward or slightly forward.

2. **Spinal Alignment:**
    - Avoid lifting the head too much or arching the back.
    - Your body should be in a straight line from head to feet.

3. **Arm and Leg Position:**
    - Your arms and legs should be relaxed but ready for movement.
    - Movements should be smooth and coordinated.

4.2 Basic Breathing Techniques

Proper breathing is crucial for comfort and efficiency in swimming.

1. **Breathing through the Mouth:**
    - In most types of swimming, it's preferable to inhale through the mouth when your head is out of the water.
2. **Exhaling in the Water:**
    - When your head is submerged, exhale slowly through your nose or mouth (or both).
    - This helps regulate your breath and prepares you for the next inhalation.
3. **Breathing Rhythm:**
    - Breathing should be regular and synchronized with your movements. For example, in freestyle swimming, you typically breathe every 3 or 5 strokes.

4.3 Balance and Buoyancy in Water

Buoyancy is a foundational skill that helps build confidence and control while swimming.

1. **Back Floating Exercise:**
    - Lie on your back with your arms and legs extended.
    - Tilt your head back slightly so your ears stay underwater and your face remains above the surface.
    - Focus on relaxing and breathing slowly.
2. **Balance in Water:**

- Balance is achieved when your weight is evenly distributed.
- Use small movements of your arms and legs to maintain stability.

4.4 Basic Exercises to Adapt to Water

To master the fundamentals of swimming, it's helpful to start with simple exercises:

1. **Walking in Water:**
   - Start by walking in a shallow area to get comfortable with the movement of the water around your body.
2. **Swimming with Arms Only:**
   - Hold onto a kickboard or the edge of the pool.
   - Move your legs up and down in a continuous motion without moving your arms.
3. **Swimming with Legs Only:**
   - Hold a kickboard in front of you with your arms extended.
   - Start moving your legs in a gentle, steady flutter kick.

4.5 Improving Buoyancy through Breathing Control

Breathing control helps improve buoyancy and reduces anxiety while swimming:

1. **Holding Air:**
    - When you inhale and hold the air in your lungs, you'll find that your body floats better.
    - Use this to enhance your buoyancy position when needed.
2. **Slow Exhalation:**
    - Once you're comfortable, start exhaling slowly underwater, then inhale when you raise your head.

4.6 Building Confidence through Repetition

Repetition is key to success in mastering swimming fundamentals. Make time for regular practice:

• **Body Position Training:** Keep working on improving your body alignment and balance in the water.

• **Underwater Breathing:** Repeat breathing and buoyancy exercises daily to enhance your performance.

• **Maintaining Comfort and Relaxation:** The goal is to reach a point where your movements feel natural and comfortable.

This chapter focuses on developing essential skills, paving the way for continuous learning and achieving swimming proficiency

Chapter 5: Learning Basic Swimming Strokes

5.1 Freestyle (Crawl)
Freestyle is one of the most popular and

beginner-friendly strokes, combining speed and efficiency.

1. **Body Position:**
    - Lie horizontally on the water's surface, keeping your body straight.
    - Keep your head in a neutral position, looking toward the pool's bottom.

2. **Arm Movement:**
    - Use one arm at a time.
    - Pull the water with your arm from front to back while extending the other arm forward.
    - Keep the movement smooth and repetitive.

3. **Leg Movement:**
    - Flutter your legs with small, quick movements.
    - Start the kick from your hips, not from your knees, to
    - conserve energy.

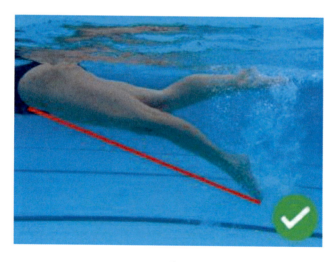

4. **Breathing:**
   - Gently turn your head to one side to take a quick breath, then return to the horizontal position.
   - Try breathing every 3 strokes to maintain rhythm.

5.2 Breaststroke

Breaststroke is a comfortable style, ideal for longer distances.

1. **Body Position:**
   - Keep your body in a slightly inclined horizontal position, with your head above the water.
2. **Arm Movement:**
   - Start by extending your arms in front of you.
   - Pull the water in a half-circular motion to the sides, bringing your hands toward your chest.
   - Extend your arms forward again.
3. **Leg Movement (Frog Kick):**
   - Bring your heels together,

　　　　　then extend your legs in a
　　　　　half-circular motion
　　　　　backward.

　　　　　○　Keep the movement
　　　　　　　coordinated with the arms.
　　4. **Breathing:**
　　　　　○　Lift your head slightly above
　　　　　　　the water during the arm
　　　　　　　pull to breathe, then lower it
　　　　　　　while extending the arms.

5.3 Backstroke

Backstroke is suitable for beginners who want to focus on body relaxation and easy breathing.

　　1. **Body Position:**
　　　　　○　Lie on your back with your
　　　　　　　face above the water.
　　　　　○　Keep your body straight and
　　　　　　　hips elevated.
　　2. **Arm Movement:**
　　　　　○　Lift one arm straight above
　　　　　　　your head, then pull it down
　　　　　　　to the water in a half-
　　　　　　　circular motion.
　　　　　○　Alternate between arms.
　　3. **Leg Movement:**

- Perform small, quick flutter kicks with your legs, maintaining knee straightness.
4. **Breathing:**
    - Breathing in backstroke is easier as your face stays above water the whole time. Breathe regularly and comfortably.

5.4 Butterfly Stroke (Simple Introduction)

Butterfly stroke is one of the most demanding styles in terms of strength and coordination. Beginners can take a simplified approach.

1. **Body Position:**
    - Keep your body horizontal, with a wave-like movement.
2. **Arm Movement:**
    - Move both arms together, pulling the water from front to back.
    - Lift your arms out of the water and return them forward.
3. **Leg Movement (Dolphin Kick):**

- Move your legs together like a dolphin's tail, with a wave-like motion starting from the hips.

4. **Breathing:**
   - Lift your head forward after every two strokes for a breath.

5.5 Improving Coordination Between Movements

To achieve greater swimming efficiency, it's essential to improve coordination between your movements:

1. **Work on Rhythm:**
   - Ensure the arm movements are synchronized with the leg movements.
   - Keep the movements smooth and coordinated for better balance.
2. **Practice Transitions:**
   - Try switching between different strokes to develop varied skills.
3. **Repetition and Review:**
   - Repetition is key to improving basic strokes.

Practice each stroke until you feel comfortable and proficient.

5.6 Using Assistive Tools
To aid in learning the strokes, you can use tools like:

- **Kickboards:** Help focus on leg movement.
- **Fins:** Enhance leg strength and help achieve smoother movements.
- **Breathing Tubes:** Help develop continuous breathing while focusing on strokes.

This chapter focuses on teaching the basic movements of different swimming strokes, helping learners build a strong foundation for further skill development.

Chapter 6: Advanced Swimming Techniques

6.1 Improving Freestyle Technique (Crawl)

After mastering the basics, you can enhance your freestyle performance by focusing on finer details.

1. **Improving Body Position:**
   - Keep your body fully extended to reduce resistance.
   - Direct your toes and hands straight ahead.
2. **Minimizing Head Movement:**
   - Avoid lifting your head excessively when breathing; only rotate it slightly to keep half of your face in the water.
   - Maintain a regular breathing rhythm (every 3 or 5 strokes).
3. **Dynamic Arm Movement:**

- Try the "high elbow pull" technique where your elbow bends well underwater.
- Accelerate the movement when your hand reaches the push phase for a stronger push.

4. **Efficient Leg Movement:**
   - Minimize excessive leg movement, keeping them stable and even, focusing on coordination with the arms.

6.2 Improving Breaststroke

Breaststroke requires focusing on the balance between strength and speed.

1. **Synchronizing Movements:**
   - Arm and leg movements should work in harmony.
   - Pull with your arms, then push with your legs at the same time before extending your arms forward again.
2. **Increasing Leg Push Power:**
   - Focus on mastering the "frog kick," ensuring it starts from the hips and ends with a full

    press on the water using the soles of your feet.
 3. **Effective Breathing:**
    - Lift your head to breathe during the arm pull, then quickly return it to the water to reduce resistance.

6.3 Improving Backstroke

Backstroke can be improved by adjusting movements and increasing efficiency.

 1. **Ideal Body Position:**
    - Ensure your hips are high enough on the water's surface.
    - Keep your gaze fixed on the ceiling to avoid tilting your head.
 2. **Arm Rotation Movement:**
    - Lift your arm straight above the water, then push it forcefully into the water.
    - Use a strong underwater pull to propel your body forward.
 3. **Continuous Flutter Kick:**
    - Start the movement from your hips, with a light, continuous leg flutter.

- Keep your knees straight to minimize resistance.

6.4 Improving Butterfly Stroke
Butterfly stroke requires strength and endurance, but it can be improved through coordination work.

1. **Mastering the Wave Motion:**
   - Focus on the wave movement that starts from the head to the feet.
   - Ensure the movements are smooth and continuous.
2. **Coordinated Arm Movement:**
   - Use both arms together to powerfully pull the water, lifting them together out of the water when returning.
3. **Breathing Timing:**
   - Breathe at the end of the arm pull, then quickly return your head to underwater to reduce resistance.

6.5 Improving Starts and Turns
Starts and turns are crucial elements in improving overall performance, especially in competitive swimming.

1. **Starting Technique:**
   - Push off strongly from the pool edge, ensuring you enter the water with your body extended and straight to minimize resistance.
   - Use the momentum to move quickly underwater before starting swimming movements.
2. **Turn Technique (Underwater Flip):**
   - When approaching the wall, execute a quick turn using your arms and feet to push off the wall powerfully.
   - Maintain your momentum as you return to your swimming position.

6.6 Strength and Endurance Training

1. **Interval Swimming Exercises:**
   - Swim short distances at high speeds with short rest periods between repetitions to improve endurance.
2. **Long-distance Swimming Workouts:**

- Swim long distances at a moderate pace to build physical stamina.
3. **Using Underwater Weights:**
    - Perform exercises using light weights underwater to increase muscular strength.

This chapter focuses on developing advanced techniques to enhance overall swimming performance and efficiency, helping learners achieve higher levels of professionalism in swimming.

Chapter 7: Swimming Safety

7.1 Importance of Safety in Swimming
Safety is one of the most important aspects that every swimmer, whether a beginner or a professional, should pay attention to. Safety rules aim to reduce risks and ensure a safe and enjoyable experience.

7.2 Identifying Swimming Hazards

1. **Drowning:**
   - Drowning is the most common risk in swimming, and it can happen due to exhaustion, panic, or inability to float.
   - It's crucial to be aware of your physical limits and not exceed them.
2. **Slips and Falls:**
   - Pool surfaces can be slippery, increasing the risk of falling and injury.
   - Walk carefully and avoid running in wet areas.
3. **Currents and Whirlpools:**
   - In open waters like seas and rivers, water currents and whirlpools can pose a significant danger.
   - It's important to recognize these hazards and stay away from unsafe areas.
4. **Sun Exposure and Heat Stress:**
   - Swimming in direct sunlight for extended periods can

lead to heat stress or sunburn.
- Use sunscreen and drink plenty of water to stay hydrated.

7.3 Pool Safety Rules

1. **Follow Lifeguard Instructions:**
   - Always follow the instructions of the pool supervisors to ensure your safety and that of others.
2. **Don't Swim Alone:**
   - Even if you are a skilled swimmer, it's always better to swim with someone else in case of an emergency.
3. **Avoid Dangerous Play:**
   - Avoid pushing others into the water or engaging in dangerous games that can lead to injury.
4. **Stick to Designated Swimming Areas:**
   - Stay within the areas designated for your skill level, whether shallow for

beginners or deep for advanced swimmers.

7.4 Open Water Safety

1. **Check Weather Conditions:**
   - Before swimming in lakes or seas, check the weather and water conditions.
   - Avoid swimming if the weather is bad or if there are warnings about strong waves.
2. **Use Safety Equipment:**
   - Wear life jackets if swimming in open or unfamiliar waters.
   - Fins or swimming boards can help improve buoyancy and reduce effort.
3. **Stay Close to the Shore:**
   - Don't swim too far from the shore so that you can easily return if you feel exhausted.

7.5 Dealing with Emergencies

1. **Stay Calm in Case of Drowning:**

- If you feel like you are drowning, try to relax and float on your back to breathe regularly.
- Use your hands to signal for help.
2. **Rescue Others Carefully:**
    - If you see someone drowning, try to help using equipment like a rope or buoy rather than getting too close, as they may pull you under.
    - Contact emergency services immediately if needed.
3. **First Aid:**
    - Learn the basics of first aid and CPR (Cardiopulmonary Resuscitation) to be prepared for emergencies.

7.6 Additional Safety Tips

- **Practice Floating and Staying Afloat:**
    - Practice staying afloat for long periods to be ready in emergencies.
- **Be Aware of Fatigue:**

- - Don't overexert yourself or swim for long periods without taking breaks.
  - If you feel tired, exit the water and rest.
- **Supervise Children:**
  - Children should always be supervised by an adult, even in shallow water.

This chapter provides the essential safety principles that every swimmer should follow to ensure a safe experience. Adhering to these guidelines can reduce risks and improve the swimmer's confidence in the water.

Chapter 8: Training Plans and Swimming Skill Development

8.1 Importance of a Training Plan

Systematic training is key to developing swimming skills, whether you are a beginner or aiming to improve your performance. A training plan ensures gradual progress and helps you achieve your goals efficiently.

8.2 Setting Goals

1. **Short-term Goals:**
   - Learn basic swimming strokes.
   - Improve buoyancy and underwater breathing.
   - Increase confidence in the water.
2. **Long-term Goals:**
   - Enhance speed and efficiency in swimming.
   - Master advanced techniques such as butterfly stroke and perfect starts.

- Participate in competitions or long-distance swimming events.

8.3 Training Plan for Beginners

1. **First Few Weeks: Getting Used to the Water**
   - Days 1-3: Buoyancy and breathing exercises.
   - Days 4-7: Leg drills using swim boards.
2. **Weeks 2 to 4: Mastering Basic Movements**
   - Freestyle and breaststroke swimming, focusing on regular breathing.
   - Balance and coordination exercises for arms and legs.
3. **Weeks 5 and Beyond: Improving Performance**
   - Gradually increase distance and speed.
   - Focus on learning backstroke and butterfly stroke.

8.4 Training Plan for Intermediate Swimmers

1. **Increasing the Challenge:**
    - Begin long-distance swimming drills to improve endurance.
    - Regular practice of starts and turns.
2. **Variety in Strokes:**
    - Include all strokes to enhance coordination and overall strength.
    - Dedicate sessions to each stroke individually.
3. **Strength and Endurance Training:**
    - Use weights and land exercises to strengthen muscles used in swimming.
    - Gradually increase training time to improve fitness.

8.5 Continuous Evaluation and Adaptation

1. **Performance Measurement:**
    - Track your progress by recording times and distances.
    - Compare your current performance with past

results to assess improvements.
2. **Adapting to Challenges:**
    - If you struggle to meet specific goals, adjust your training plan to match your progress level.
    - Add new exercises to avoid monotony and keep yourself motivated.

8.6 Tips for Self-Motivation

1. **Celebrate Small Achievements:**
    - Every improvement deserves recognition, whether it's learning a new stroke or enhancing your speed.
2. **Swim with a Partner or Group:**
    - Swimming with others can be fun and motivating, and it offers opportunities to exchange tips.
3. **Set Personal Rewards:**
    - Reward yourself for achieving goals, like purchasing new swim gear.

8.7 Seeking Professional Coaching
If you're aiming to significantly improve or compete in races, working with a coach can have a huge impact.

1. **Benefits of Personal Coaching:**
    - A coach can correct technical mistakes and provide immediate feedback.
    - They help design a personalized training plan tailored to your level and goals.
2. **Choosing the Right Coach:**
    - Look for a certified coach with experience in training swimmers at your level.
    - Ensure the coach emphasizes both safety and performance improvement.

8.8 Swimming as Part of a Healthy Lifestyle

1. **Health Benefits of Swimming:**
    - Improves cardiovascular and respiratory fitness.
    - Strengthens muscles and enhances flexibility.

- Reduces stress and promotes mental health.
2. **Combining Swimming with Other Activities:**
    - Alongside swimming, you can incorporate other exercises like running or yoga to boost overall fitness.
3. **Maintaining Balance:**
    - Make swimming a part of your daily or weekly routine to ensure progress and achieve long-term goals.

This chapter focuses on how to design an effective training plan to develop swimming skills, with an emphasis on motivation and continuous evaluation to achieve sustainable progress.

Conclusion: The Path to Mastery and Enjoyment in Swimming

Swimming is one of the most comprehensive and beneficial sports for both the body and the mind. It combines physical exercise, mental relaxation, and the joy of connecting with water. Throughout this guide, we have covered the steps of learning to swim for beginners, from getting accustomed to the water, mastering basic strokes, to acquiring advanced techniques.

The Importance of Gradual Learning
It is essential for learners to understand that swimming is not just a sport but a skill that requires patience and progression. The journey always starts with mastering the basics and building confidence in the water, before advancing to more

complex techniques. Continuous repetition and regular practice are the keys to progress and mastery.

Safety Comes First and Always
Safety is not just a section in this guide but a foundational element in every step of learning to swim. Adhering to safety guidelines, whether in pools or open waters, protects you from potential risks and ensures a safe and enjoyable experience. Always remember that awareness and vigilance are your first line of defense in the water.

Swimming as Part of a Healthy Lifestyle
As you advance in your swimming journey, you will discover its physical and mental health benefits. Swimming strengthens muscles, improves heart and lung functions, and helps reduce stress. It also

boosts self-confidence and nurtures a sense of accomplishment.

Continuity and Development
Learning never stops; swimming is a sport filled with challenges and opportunities for growth. Whether you aim to improve your speed, learn new strokes, or participate in competitions, the possibilities for further development are endless. Continuous training, using helpful tools, and learning from others' experiences will always contribute to your improvement.

A Final Word
Swimming is not just a skill to be acquired; it is a journey to be enjoyed every step of the way. No matter your goal—whether for recreation, fitness, or competition—water will always be a wonderful partner in achieving these objectives. So, enjoy your journey and always be ready to

explore new depths in the world of swimming.

We hope this comprehensive guide has provided you with the support and guidance you need to confidently embark on this aquatic adventure. Now, it's time to put on your swimsuit and dive into an enjoyable and safe experience!

Made in the USA
Middletown, DE
16 July 2025